Danceball

To Pro FootBall

Steve Bird

Table of Contents

Dedication

To all those who believe they can't..you can.

Acknowledgment

To my wife and children for believing in me, to Mujtaba Aly and his team for all your support and patience along the way...!! To turning it from a dream to reality, hope to work with you again in the future.

About the Author

Just an average bloke, who grew up on a local council estate who decided to have a go at writing a book, if I can do it anyone can.

Chapter 1

This is a tale about two young boys who were born with a lot of talent — one with his feet, the other with his hands. The boy with the gift in his feet was called Steve, and his brother Luke was blessed with speed and precision in his hands. Both were ordinary boys on the surface, but there was something extraordinary stirring within them, something that neither of them, nor anyone else, could fully see yet.

Their story began in the rougher end of a small northern town, a place where the houses were packed tightly together, and where the streetlamps were faulty, so they turned on and off most nights. The smell of coal smoke and cheap lager seemed to hang in the air, and dreams, like the clouds, were often grey or blue. For Steve and Luke, childhood was much less about enjoying the feeling of being young and more about surviving each day as it came.

Their father, **Arthur**, had once been a decent man by most accounts. He would work down at the docks, where his hands had grown calloused, and his back had bent from long hours hauling crates. But when the docks closed, Arthur's sense of pride closed with them. Work became harder to find, the money ran thin, and the pub became his only refuge. It started with a pint or two after a long day. Then the pints became nights, and the nights became debts, and soon everything blurred into one another.

Arthur was not an evil man, but weakness can be just as dangerous. The local bookmakers knew him well; he was the kind who always thought his luck would change next week. And when it didn't, he borrowed to keep chasing that impossible win. At first, it was small loans. He would borrow a few quid from mates or the corner shop owner. But the kind of people willing to lend to desperate men weren't friends for long.

Steve and Luke's mother, **Margaret**, had warned him. She had seen the shadow settling over him long before it took full shape. "You're gambling with more than money, Arthur," she'd said once, after finding another pawn slip tucked under the mattress. "You're gambling with us."

He had looked at her, shame flooding his tired eyes, but still couldn't stop. The debts piled up faster than he could pay them, and soon people started talking about him. Not the sort of people whom you want to talk about you. The kind of men who never forgot a debt.

One bitterly cold evening, when the frost crept up the windows and the wind howled through the alleyways, they came without much of an announcement. Steve and Luke were asleep in the small room they shared, their thin blankets pulled tight. Margaret had just sat down with a cup of tea when there was a hard and loud knock at the door. She knew something was wrong as soon as she heard the banging.

When she opened it, three men stood on the doorstep. One tall, one short, and one who said nothing at all, but whose stare could freeze your blood. Arthur stood behind her, pale and trembling.

"You know why we're here," said the tall one.

Arthur nodded. "I—I just need more time. I'll have it next week, I swear."

But there was no more time left. The short one laughed. He knew very well that Arthur's time was over, and it was useless to ask for any further extensions.

That night, Arthur went with them. Margaret had begged them to leave him be, to give him another chance, but her words fell flat against their cold faces. Steve had woken up just in time to see his father being led away down the street, the men's dark coats flapping behind them. He never saw him again.

A few days later, the police found Arthur's body floating in the river. The official report said, "accidental drowning", but no one in that town believed it. The river had become the kind of place where debts were settled behind the scenes.

The men came back not long after, and this time, they weren't after Arthur. They wanted what was left. They wanted the house, the furniture, anything that could be turned into money. Margaret stood her ground at first. "You've taken enough from us," she said, holding Luke and Steve behind her. But the tall man simply smiled, knowing fully well that she was completely powerless before them.

"You've got two fine boys there," he said. "Be a shame if something happened to them, too."

That was all it took. With shaking hands, Margaret signed over the deeds to the house, her name scribbled on the line that stripped away everything she had. The men took the papers, nodded to one another, and left, leaving the family with nothing but their clothes and a few boxes of old memories.

With nothing left, they had to leave. There was no time to look back at what once was their home, no time to mourn over the shattered windows or the broken pieces of furniture left behind.

Their mother carried a single torn suitcase that rattled with what little they had salvaged: a few clothes, an old photograph of their father before the bottle claimed him, and a rusted locket that had belonged to her own mother.

Luke, the elder by just two years, trudged alongside her, trying to stay strong. He learned early that his mother hated to see him cry. Steve, younger and quieter, walked barefoot through puddles, his toes gripping the cold pavement. Their reality had shifted from right underneath them.

"Where are we going?" Luke asked, his small voice trembling in the cold air.

His mother didn't look back. "Away from all this," she said softly. "So, you and Steve don't have to deal with what the world is like around bad people in life."

There was something in her tone, a bitterness that Luke didn't yet understand. She had seen too much. She had seen too many men like her husband. All she wanted now was distance. Distance from the noise, the bars, the men in dark coats who knocked at her door with threats disguised as business.

They walked until their feet blistered. The city lights faded into the horizon behind them, swallowed by the mist of the countryside. It was late, and the rain had grown heavier, drumming against their coats like impatient fingers. That's when they came upon an old building. It was a crumbling shell of brick and wood that might once have been a warehouse or a boarding house. Its roof sagged, and the windows were mostly gone, but to a family with nowhere else to go, it looked like a sanctuary.

"Let's go in," Mother said, pulling the boys close. The rain had soaked through her thin dress, and she shivered as they crossed the threshold.

Inside, the air was musty, filled with the scent of old wood and damp concrete. They found a small room at the back where the floor was mostly dry. A broken table lay against one wall, and a pile of discarded cloth sat in the corner—perhaps left behind by another wanderer.

"Are we staying now, Mother?" Steve asked, hugging himself against the chill.

"We will see," she replied, though her voice betrayed no real hope. She didn't want to promise safety in a world that kept taking it away.

The three of them sat close together, sharing the single blanket she carried. The wind outside howled through cracks in the walls, and the rain whispered against the roof. For a brief moment, Steve thought he heard laughter—his father's laughter—from somewhere far away, the kind that used to echo through the house before everything turned sour. He closed his eyes to block it out.

Then they heard footsteps. The fear kicked in with each step of the boot.

"Mum, there's someone outside the door," Luke said, his heart pounding.

Steve's small body tensed. He backed into the corner, eyes wide with fear. Their mother stood, her hand trembling as she reached for a piece of broken wood, her only weapon.

The footsteps stopped. Silence.

Then, the doorknob turned.

"Boys, come here now!" she commanded, her voice cutting through the stillness. The boys obeyed instantly, clinging to her skirt as the door creaked open.

For a moment, no one moved.

Standing in the doorway was an old woman, her face lined with years and stories untold. Her eyes, pale and sharp as glass, darted between them. Her hair was silver, tied back in a bun, and she wore a tattered shawl over her shoulders.

"Well," she said in a surprisingly calm voice, "have I got company tonight?"

Their mother lowered the wood slightly, still cautious. "We didn't mean to intrude," she said. "We just needed a place out of the rain."

The old woman smiled faintly. "You chose well. This building hasn't seen life in years. Not since the factory closed. Come in properly, child. No one should be left out on a night like this."

Her tone was full of a strange, tender warmth, something that made the boys relax, even as their mother hesitated. After a short conversation, they agreed to stay the night.

That one night turned into a week. Then a month. Then years.

The old woman, whose name was Miss Wren, became something like family. She lived in that building by choice, away from the noise of the world. No one quite knew where she came from, and she never offered the story. But she saw something in Luke and Steve. It was something rare.

She noticed how Luke's hands moved faster than the eye could follow, how he could catch falling objects before they touched the ground, fix broken things with precision and speed. She noticed how Steve, though smaller, had remarkable balance, how his feet seemed to dance even when he wasn't trying to.

"They've got gifts," Miss Wren told their mother one evening as they sat by the small fire they'd built from scrap wood. "Don't waste them. The world may have taken everything from you, but these boys still have something that can't be stolen."

And so began the years of training.

Luke, being the older, took to physical tasks quickly. Miss Wren would make him run through the hallways, dodging swinging ropes and obstacles she set up from broken furniture. "Speed is nothing without purpose," she'd say. "Use it to defend, not to destroy."

Steve's lessons were different. They were about control and precision. Things like how to move silently, how to balance on narrow ledges, how to turn fear into focus. "Your feet are your anchor," Miss Wren told him. "They'll take you anywhere, if you learn to trust them."

Their mother worked odd jobs in nearby towns, cleaning and mending clothes for a few coins, while the boys grew stronger under Miss Wren's guidance. Over ten years, they changed from frightened children into young men with confidence in their movements and quiet fire in their hearts.

By the time Luke turned seventeen, he could move faster than most men could think. When fights broke out, sometimes with thieves or drifters who came to the old building, his opponents rarely landed a blow. His hands were a blur, his body moving with instinct and precision. Steve, though younger, was just as formidable, able to leap, dodge, and strike with fluid grace.

Despite everything that had happened, Margaret never let bitterness consume her. "Your father made mistakes," she told them one night as they sat around a flickering candle during a power cut, "but you don't have to. You can be better than what this world gave you."

And they listened. They always listened.

Chapter 2

For a while, life seemed to quiet down. The years under Miss Wren's care had been hard but filled with purpose, and both boys had grown into capable young men with strong hearts and calloused hands. But the peace was short-lived.

Their mother, who had always been the anchor between them and the chaos of the world, began to grow frail. It started, as it often does, with simple tiredness. She would rest longer by the fire or cough quietly into her sleeve. But soon, her strength faded faster than any of them could understand. Miss Wren did her best to care for her, mixing strange herbal brews and old remedies she claimed came from her grandmother. But the sickness would not be undone.

For weeks, the little family lived under a cloud of worry. Luke often stayed up at night, listening to his mother's uneven breathing, while Steve sat by her side, holding her hand and whispering that everything would be all right. They were all waiting. Waiting for something to happen as they sat in the smell of damp wood and despair.

Margaret tried to reassure her sons, even as her strength slipped away. "You boys are strong," she'd say with a weak smile. "Stronger than you know. Whatever happens, you've got each other, and that's more than most."

Then, one morning, she didn't wake up.

It was Luke who found her. She was still and quiet beneath her worn blanket, the morning light spilling across her face through the cracks in the boarded-up window. He did not cry, not at first. He just stood there as the world around him shifted from underneath his feet. Steve, when he realised, clung to his brother, sobbing uncontrollably. The woman who had carried them through every storm was gone.

Miss Wren took charge of what little ceremony they could manage. She wrapped Margaret in a simple cloth, and together the three of them carried her down to the edge of the nearby woods. They dug a grave beneath an old oak tree, the roots curling around them like arms. Steve laid a small white stone at the foot of the grave, one he had found years ago near the river — smooth, with a line running through it like a scar.

After that, something in both boys hardened. They had lost too much already to be children any longer.

But fate wasn't finished with them yet. Only a few months later, Miss Wren herself fell ill. She had hidden her frailty from them for as long as she could, insisting she was only tired. But the winter was cruel that year. The cold seeped into her bones, and one evening, as the wind howled through the cracks in the roof, she too slipped quietly away.

When they found her, she was still sitting in her chair by the fire, as if she had simply drifted off to sleep.

The boys buried her beside their mother, the earth damp beneath their feet. They stood in silence for a long time, as they heard the sound of the wind rustling through the trees.

"What do we do now?" Steve asked. It was just the two of them now.

Luke looked at the two graves, then up at the sky.

"We keep going," he said quietly. "That's what they'd want."

They were alone now. Truly alone.

For a few days, they stayed in the old building, trying to hold on to what little warmth remained. The silence was soon starting to become unbearable. Every little empty creak across the hallway reminded them of the people who were no longer there. Luke knew they couldn't stay. They had no food, no firewood, and the cold would soon be too much for them to bear.

"Come on, Steve," he said one morning, shouldering the old rucksack Miss Wren had once used for foraging. "We need to find somewhere else to stay."

Steve nodded, though his stomach ached with hunger. They packed what little they had left — a few crumbs of stale bread, a flask of water, and the locket their mother had always worn — and left the only home they had ever really known.

They walked for miles through fields and half-forgotten roads, the world around them grey and tired. By the second day, their food was gone. Hunger gnawed at their insides like a cruel animal.

"Luke," Steve said weakly, "I'm hungry."

"I know, little brother. Just hold on a bit longer."

They passed through a small market town by the third evening. The smell of roasted meat and fresh bread hung in the air, torturing them. The stalls were closing, the traders packing up for the night, their baskets filled with fruit and loaves and coins. Luke hesitated at the edge of the square, looking at Steve's pale face.

"I don't want to," Steve said softly.

"I know. But we don't have a choice."

They slipped into the market shadows. Luke grabbed a loaf of bread from a cart when the vendor turned away, tossing it to Steve. But before they could run, a hand seized Luke's collar. The vendor shouted, and within seconds, others joined in. The boys tried to flee, but hunger had weakened them.

They were caught.

The next thing they knew, they were standing before a stern-looking officer in a dark coat. He asked them questions they could barely answer. Where were their parents? Who was looking after them? The answers came out broken and confused. Margaret and Miss Wren were gone. The boys had no one left.

So, the state took over.

Luke and Steve were placed into care. They were separated, despite their protests. Luke was sent to a facility in one part of the county, Steve to another. They promised it would only be temporary, that they'd be reunited soon, but weeks turned into months. The boys' lives diverged like two branches from the same tree, growing in different directions.

Steve's new foster family lived in a small, neat house on the edge of town. They were kind enough. It was a middle-aged couple, Martin and Elaine, who had two children of their own. They loved football. Every weekend, they watched matches together on the television, cheering and arguing over players and teams.

That first Saturday, as Steve sat on the sofa watching the match, his eyes followed the players with fascination. The way the ball moved, the way the game seemed to flow — it reminded him of the drills Miss Wren used to make him do, the way she had taught him to trust his movement.

"I can do that," he said suddenly.

Martin chuckled. "Can you, now?"

"Yes. Have you got a ball?"

"As a matter of fact, we do," said Martin's son, grinning. "Out in the garden."

Steve went outside. The grass was wet, but that didn't stop him. He started juggling the ball, tapping it between his feet, keeping it in the air effortlessly. His movements were smooth and natural, almost hypnotic. Within moments, the other boy ran inside.

"Dad! Dad, you need to see this! He's better than the players on TV!"

Martin came out, expecting to humour his son, and then he froze. Steve was dancing with the ball between his legs, flicking it up, catching it on his foot, and then sending it spinning into the air before trapping it perfectly again. It looked effortless, like the ball belonged to him.

"Where's my phone?" Martin shouted, running back inside.

His wife looked up from the kitchen sink. "Why?"

"Because I need to film this! You've got to see him. Elaine, he's incredible!"

Elaine followed him out just as he started recording. "He's that good?" she asked sceptically.

"Better," Martin said, eyes wide. "The ball sticks to his feet like it's glued there. This kid's special."

Elaine watched for a moment and slowly nodded. "Then we need to help him. Someone should see this. A coach, a scout, someone who knows talent when they see it."

Martin wasted no time. That evening, he called the local football club, insisting they needed to see the boy play. They were polite but dismissive, until he sent them the video.

An hour later, they called back. "We need your address," the coach said.

"I'll give it to you," Martin replied, "but I'll have to speak with Social Services first. He's in foster care, and I want to make sure it's done properly."

Social Services approved the idea. They said it could help Steve's development, as long as he was safe and happy.

When Martin told him the news, Steve's face lit up but then fell slightly. "I can't do anything until I speak to Luke," he said. "He's my big brother. Mum told me to always do what Luke says."

"Where is he?" Martin asked gently.

Steve looked down. "I don't know."

Martin's heart ached at the sadness in the boy's voice. The next day, he called Social Services again, asking if they knew where Luke was. The social worker sighed, explaining that Luke had been moved between homes, and they were still trying to find him.

"I'll find him," she promised. "He deserves to be with his brother."

A week later, the phone rang. It was the same social worker. "We've located Luke," she said. "It didn't work out with his last carers, so we're trying to find him a new placement."

Martin hesitated, then said, "What about me and my wife fostering both of them?"

There was a pause on the other end, then a moment of consideration, followed by a reply. "Leave it with me," she said.

Martin hung up and turned to Elaine, who was standing by the doorway, hopeful. "They might let us take both of them," he said quietly.

Elaine smiled. "Then let's make sure they finally have a home."

For the first time in years, there was hope again for the boys.

Chapter 3

eanwhile, life began to settle into a new kind of rhythm for Steve. Training with the local football team had become the high-light of his days, and it didn't take long for everyone there to realise he was something extraordinary. The moment he stepped onto the pitch, the other boys noticed it. Despite being young, he moved with the confidence of an adult player. It was almost as if the ball seemed to obey him as if it were an extension of his own body.

At first, they thought it was luck. A trick of the eye. But after a few sessions, even the most seasoned players on the youth squad stopped what they were doing just to watch him. His footwork was smooth, lightning quick, and almost artistic, like someone dancing with the wind at their heels. Miss Wren's early lessons, the drills in the abandoned hall, the way she would clap her hands to a beat while Steve switched feet, all of it lived in him still.

The team manager, a broad-shouldered man named Mr Hale, found himself smiling every time Steve touched the ball. He had coached talented kids before, but none like this.

One afternoon, after a particularly impressive training session where Steve weaved through six players as if they were standing still, Mr Hale put a hand on his shoulder.

"Son," he said, shaking his head in disbelief, "I've been doing this job for twenty-five years, and I've never seen feet like yours. We'd love for you to sign a contract with us... officially join the team."

But Steve stepped back slightly, clutching his water bottle tightly. "I can't," he said quietly.

Mr Hale blinked. "Why not?"

"I can't sign anything without my big brother Luke knowing," Steve said. "He always decides the serious stuff. It's how it's been since we were little."

There was something in his voice, something that was a mix of loyalty, fear, and love, that told Mr Hale the conversation was over for now.

"We'll respect that," he said. "And don't worry, Steve. When Luke gets here, I'll make sure he knows how good you are. And as for him... well, this is a football camp, but I might know just the place for a lad who's good with his hands."

Before Steve could ask what he meant, Mr Hale's phone began to ring. He pulled it from his pocket, glanced at the screen, and raised an eyebrow.

"It's your foster dad," he said, stepping aside to take the call.

The conversation lasted longer than Steve expected. Mr Hale's face shifted through several expressions. At first, he looked curious, then concerned, then surprised all of a sudden, until he finally resolved into a grin.

He hung up the phone and walked back toward Steve.

"Steve," he said, "I've got news. Good news."

"What?" Steve asked, tense.

"It's about Luke." Mr Hale's smile grew warm. "He's coming to join you at home. You'll be together again."

For a moment, Steve's face didn't move. Then his eyes filled with tears that came faster than he could wipe them away.

Mr Hale knelt down. "Hey — why are you crying?"

"It's nothing," Steve sobbed. "It's just... me and Luke... before all this, we'd never spent a night apart."

Mr Hale rested a gentle hand on his shoulder. He didn't say anything else; he didn't need to. Some emotions just needed to be felt, heard, and processed, without any words hanging in the air to dilute them.

*

A few days later, Luke arrived at the foster home carrying a small bag and wearing the same guarded expression he had learned to hide behind in the care system. But the moment he saw Steve waiting by the door, all the hardness melted away. Steve launched himself into his brother's arms, and Luke held him tight, refusing to let go for several long seconds.

Martin, whom Luke had only known as "the foster father", stood nearby, smiling. Elaine wiped her eyes discreetly with the corner of her sleeve.

"You ready to see the training ground?" Martin asked once the brothers finally separated.

Luke nodded, and the next day they all drove down together.

The pitch buzzed with activity: shouts, whistles, the loud thud of footballs being kicked. Steve ran ahead, excited to introduce his brother, while Luke hung back, taking everything in. He'd never been on a proper training ground before.

When they met Mr Hale, the manager wasted no time.

"So," he said, looking Luke up and down, "you really want to know if your brother's good enough to play?"

Luke shrugged, half-smiling. "I know he's good. But what do you think?"

"Most definitely," Mr Hale said with a breathless chuckle. "In my whole career, I've never seen someone like him. Your little brother... he's the real deal."

Luke's chest swelled with pride, though he tried to hide it. "When we were younger, Steve also loved to dance," he added. "We made up a game we played for years. If you think he's good now, try playing music while he trains. You won't believe what he can do."

Mr Hale raised his eyebrows. "Is that right?"

"It is," Luke nodded.

Moments later, music echoed across the pitch. And as soon as the beat hit, Steve changed into a different person altogether. His movements sharpened, flowed, and rose with confidence. His feet tapped out patterns in perfect time with the music. He spun past defenders, flicked the ball up onto his shoulder, and sent it rolling down his back before catching it mid-step. The entire team watched in stunned silence.

Mr Hale fumbled for his phone.

"I need to call the chairman," he muttered. "We need to sign this kid fast."

*

Meanwhile, Luke was getting to know the other players, especially a tall boy named Callum who seemed to know everything about every gym within twenty miles.

"You box, right?" Callum asked, noticing the way Luke's hands were wrapped in tape beneath his sleeves.

"Used to," Luke said. "Haven't trained properly in a while."

"You should come with me," Callum said. "The local gym has real fighters. Proper coaches, too."

Luke felt a spark inside. It was something familiar, something that belonged to the part of him Miss Wren helped shape. But before he could say yes, he knew there was a process.

"I need to ask permission first," he said. "My foster dad will have to check with Social Services at our meeting this afternoon."

Callum shrugged. "Fair enough. Hope it works out."

When training ended, Luke jogged over to Steve. "Come on, Steve, Dad is waiting for us."

Steve blinked. "Dad?"

"Yes," Luke said. "Dad. He's now our dad, Steve," then he paused for a second, "If you're okay with calling him that."

Steve frowned thoughtfully. "Wonderful. But we should ask him first, just to be sure."

Back at the house, they explained it to Martin, who was stunned for a moment before his eyes softened.

"You boys can call me Dad," he said. "And Elaine would be honoured to be called Mum. After all,... we're hoping to adopt you both."

Steve gasped. Luke looked away quickly, pretending to study the wallpaper so no one would notice the sudden gloss in his eyes.

For the first time in a long time, the world felt safe again.

*

Later that afternoon, the social worker arrived and went over their placement details, the boys' development, and their emotional progress. When Luke mentioned the boxing gym, she listened carefully.

"I think it could be good for him," Martin said. "Structure, discipline... something he enjoys."

Steve nodded eagerly. "Luke's really good. Miss Wren said he had quick hands. Faster than most grown-ups."

The social worker smiled. "All right. As long as the gym is reputable and supervised, Luke can join."

Luke felt something light inside him, something letting go of the weight he had unconsciously been holding on to.

After the meeting, Martin ruffled his hair. "Ready to work on your own talent then, champ?"

Luke grinned, the faintest spark of confidence igniting in his eyes.

"Yeah," he said. "I'm ready."

The brothers walked into the house together, side by side, no longer alone. They had a home again, people who cared, and roads ahead that finally led somewhere brighter. Steve had football. Luke had boxing. And both had each other.

For the first time since losing their mother and Miss Wren, the future didn't feel like something to fear. It was something they could grow into. Together.

Chapter 4

Word about Steve had begun spreading far beyond the local pitches and weekend matches. Clips of him weaving through players like a gust of wind, the ball clinging to his feet as if it were enchanted, had circulated among coaches, scouts, and even a few retired professionals who still kept an eye on promising youth talent. His name drifted from one conversation to another, until it gathered enough momentum to echo across the wider football world. People were curious. Some were extremely sceptical. Others excited. But all were waiting to see if the stories were true.

To test the rumours, a friendly match was arranged between Steve's youth team and a well-established, highly respected club known for producing some of the country's finest players. It was an extraordinary opportunity. Almost unheard of for someone of Steve's age, but the chairman of the club had watched the recording Mr Hale had sent and insisted on seeing the boy himself.

On the day of the match, the stadium buzzed with an energy far bigger than a simple friendly should have carried. Parents filled the stands. Coaches from other clubs were gathered near the rails. Even a few scouts tried to blend into the crowd, pretending to be casual onlookers. But everyone knew why they were there.

Steve didn't start the match. The manager had decided it was best to protect him from the pressure and expectations of the roaring crowd. Instead, Steve sat on the bench, quiet but alert, his eyes following every pass, every run, every mistake his team made with an intensity beyond his years.

By the time the second half began, Steve's team was down 2–0. The opposing side looked sharper, stronger, more experienced. It felt like the kind of game that was slipping away fast.

Then, with twenty minutes left on the clock, Mr Hale gave a small nod toward Steve.

"You're on," he said gently. "Play your game. Nothing more."

Steve swallowed, nodded, and jogged onto the pitch.

The atmosphere shifted the moment his boots touched the grass. The first time the ball reached him, two defenders closed in. Steve didn't panic. He tapped the ball gently with the inside of his foot, spinning it behind him with a smoothness that made the closest defender stumble. In a flash, he had passed both of them.

Within three minutes, Steve curled a shot past the keeper. 2–1.

The crowd erupted.

Five minutes later, he slipped a perfectly timed pass through a gap so narrow even older players wouldn't have attempted it. His teammate tapped it in. 2–2.

All the talk of disbelief turned into full-throated cheers.

Then came the third goal. It was Steve stealing the ball at midfield, sprinting with electrifying speed, dancing past a defender with a step-over so clean it left the boy frozen. He finished with a powerful strike. 3–2.

The fourth goal was almost unfair. A defender shoved him off balance, but Steve kept control of the ball, cutting inside and firing low into the bottom corner. 4–2.

Two more assists followed, and each was a display of awareness and maturity that coaches rarely saw even in professional-level youth players. By the time the final whistle blew, the scoreboard read 6–2.

The stadium didn't simply cheer. They stood. They applauded. They shouted his name like they were witnessing the birth of someone destined for greatness.

But Steve didn't celebrate wildly. He looked almost shy, glancing around as if unsure how to react to the tidal wave of attention. After the match ended, Mr Hale walked straight to him, placed a steady arm around his shoulders, and quietly guided him toward the tunnel.

"Come with me, son," he whispered. "Let's get you inside."

Inside the dressing room, the lights blinked gently, and the air was much cooler and calmer. The sounds of the crowd faded into a soft murmur behind the thick walls. Steve sat on a bench, still catching his breath, his cheeks flushed red, not from exhaustion, but from everything happening faster than his mind could process.

Mr Hale crouched in front of him. "Stay in here until your dad arrives," he said. "You've done something incredible today, and people are going to want things from you. Pictures, interviews, promises. You're too young for all that. You don't need that weight yet."

Steve nodded. He was grateful for the quiet. Grateful for the space to breathe.

A few minutes later, Martin—already Dad in the boys' hearts—arrived at the dressing room door, escorted by a staff member. When he walked in and saw Steve sitting quietly, his expression softened.

"Thank you," Martin said to the manager, voice thick with emotion. "Thank you for looking after him."

Mr Hale shook his head. "He's special, Martin. But he's still a kid, and he needs protecting. We'll make sure he gets that."

Steve stood and walked toward his dad, who embraced him tightly, tighter than he had ever expected from someone who hadn't known him long. In that hug, Steve felt something he hadn't felt since the days with Miss Wren. It was a sense of promise for a future.

Having talent was a blessing, but it wasn't everything. Martin understood something that many people in the sports world often forgot: raw ability could open doors, but education would keep those doors open. He knew what it meant to grow up without stability, without guidance, without anyone reminding you that the world was bigger than hardship. He didn't want Steve and Luke to become just stories of talent lost or potential wasted. He wanted them to have a foundation, one that their late mother never had the chance to build.

So, as they were leaving the stadium, Martin approached Steve's manager.

"I appreciate everything you're doing for him," Martin began, "but I want to make sure both boys get an education, too. Something steady.

Something that'll hold them up no matter what happens in football or boxing."

The manager smiled, as if relieved to hear a father speak with such clarity.

"Of course," he replied. "We can help. We've got partnerships with schools that support young athletes. We'll make sure both boys get the right balance."

And with that, another piece of their new life clicked into place.

A few days later, the manager arranged for one of the older players—Josh, a disciplined midfielder who had spent years balancing schoolwork with football—to take Luke to the local gym. The idea wasn't just for training; it was also to give Luke a sense of belonging, a place to channel the restless energy he carried, shaped by years of running, surviving, and protecting his little brother.

Naturally, Steve wanted to come too. They had spent nearly every day of their lives with each other; the idea of being separated now, even for an hour, didn't sit right.

Luke held out a hand to him. "Come on then."

Martin chuckled. "Alright, both of you. But you're there to watch, Steve. No climbing into rings unless someone tells me first."

When they stepped into the gym, the atmosphere felt completely different from the football training grounds. Instead of fresh-cut grass and open sky, there were punching bags thudding rhythmically, the warm smell of leather gloves, the shine of polished boxing shoes gliding across worn mats, and men shouting encouragement from every corner.

The gym owner was a broad-shouldered man with a deep voice and years etched into every line on his face, whom Luke noticed immediately.

"So," he said, sizing him up with a practised eye, "you're the kid with the fast hands?"

Luke nodded, though his posture remained tense. This was different from the streets, different from the improvised training the old woman had given him in the abandoned building they once called home. Here, everything felt official. Serious and real, no space to mess around.

"Well then," the owner continued, slapping his hands together, "let's see it. Go get gloved up, and we'll put you in the ring."

Luke hesitated only long enough to glance at Steve, then disappeared into the back where the gloves were stored. Steve, meanwhile, scanned the gym and immediately noticed something wrong.

"Dad... he's too small," Steve said under his breath. "The old lady taught us, never fight someone smaller than you."

Martin looked at the boy in the opposite corner. He was lean, maybe a year younger, and clearly not expecting anything dramatic from the spar.

The gym owner waved a dismissive hand. "It'll be fine. Just a light spar. I wanna see the lad's speed."

But Steve shook his head, that protective instinct rising in him like a reflex. Luke may have been the older one, but Steve had always acted like a shield, always looking, always assessing the dangers around them.

"Luke," Steve said quietly as his brother walked toward the ring, "just be careful."

"I will," Luke replied. "Promise."

They touched gloves. The bell rang.

And then everything ended in less than a second.

Luke stepped forward, twisted his torso the way Miss Wren had taught him, and launched a punch so fast the air split around it. The smaller boy dropped instantly, his legs giving way like he'd been unplugged from reality.

The gym fell silent.

One of the trainers rushed to the fallen boy, who was dazed but conscious. The gym owner turned slowly toward Luke, eyes wide, mouth hanging slightly open.

"Dear God..." he muttered. "Where did you learn that?"

Luke, breathing steadily, simply shrugged. "We used to train. The old lady who looked after us... she taught me a lot."

The owner shook his head in disbelief. "Kid, you're not fast. You're lightning. That punch, I've seen professionals who can't throw like that.

He turned to Martin with a rare seriousness. "Sir, I want to train this boy. Properly. If he stays at it, he could go professional in a year. Maybe less."

Luke's face lit up like he was seeing his whole future opening in front of him. "Dad, please. Please let me do it. I want this. I know I can do it."

Martin held up a hand gently. "Luke, slow down. Something like this... You don't jump into it without talking to your mum first."

Luke deflated slightly, but the hopeful, eager smile stayed plastered on his face.

"We'll talk to her," Martin continued. "Both of us. Tonight. And if she agrees... then we'll see."

The gym owner nodded respectfully. "Fair enough. But don't take too long. This boy is something special."

As they left the gym, Luke bounced on his toes the entire walk home, shadowboxing imaginary opponents, the joy practically radiating from him. Steve watched with a smile, feeling a warmth he hadn't felt in years: the feeling of seeing his brother happy, safe, and dreaming bigger than survival.

At home, Dad spoke with Mum, whilst the boys listened with their ears pressed right up against the door, the same way they had done countless times back in the old building with the old lady. Some habits stayed with you, even when life finally felt safe.

"I don't know," Mum said softly, her voice tight with worry. "They are still young."

The boys exchanged anxious looks. They could practically feel Mum's hesitation leaking through the wood of the door. Luke nudged Steve, and Steve nudged him back, both silently arguing about who would be the brave one to push the door open. In the end, they did it together.

"We can do it!" Steve and Luke shouted in unison as they burst into the room.

Mum nearly jumped from her chair. Dad turned around with the smallest of smiles, as if he had known all along, they were there, listening, waiting.

"I see you are both very excited about this," Mother replied, trying to hide the flicker of amusement behind her concern.

"We sure are!" the boys said, breathless, the words tumbling out as though their dreams depended on the speed of their answers.

Luke stood firmly, shoulders squared like he was already stepping into a boxing ring, ready for whatever came next. Steve stood beside him, bouncing on the balls of his feet the way he always did when something important was at stake. It was clear: training wasn't just a hobby for them. It was a doorway to a future they hadn't dared imagine back when they used to sleep in cold rooms and dodge trouble out on the streets.

Mother looked between them. It reminded her of how she had fought for them; how much struggle she had put up against agencies and courts just to keep them together. Maybe... maybe this was their turn to fight for something that mattered.

"All right," she finally said, exhaling slowly. "I'll agree. But only on one condition: both of you must receive a proper education while you train. No arguments."

"That is already in hand," Dad said confidently, stepping forward as though he had been waiting for that moment. "Luke's manager and Steve's coach have arranged for tutoring sessions at the training grounds. They'll make sure the boys stay on track. They're both willing to help however they can."

Mother's shoulders softened, some of the weight lifted from her expression. "Good," she replied. "Then... I suppose there's nothing left to worry about."

"There's loads to worry about," Dad chuckled, "but none of it is more important than giving them a chance."

The boys beamed, feeling like things were finally starting to fit into place. They were no longer surviving from day to day. They were building something.

Steve rushed forward and wrapped his arms around Mum's waist. "Thank you," he said, voice muffled against her jumper.

Luke wasn't far behind, hugging her with equal strength, though he tried to pretend he wasn't emotional. Mum stroked the tops of their heads, a warmth spreading through her hands.

Dad watched with a smile, proud and relieved. Proud that the boys had finally found something to believe in, and relieved that he and Mum could give them what they never had before: stability and opportunity.

"All right, you two," Dad said gently. "Tomorrow starts a new chapter. Training, studying, and working hard. No slacking."

"Yes, Dad!" they chimed together, louder than necessary, overflowing with joy at the word *Dad*.

Mum looked at Dad, and for a moment, both parents—new parents, but parents all the same—shared the same thought:

This family, unexpected as it was, was becoming whole.

Chapter 5

— ★ —

With the boys now fully under the care of Social Services, life settled into a new and predictable kind of rhythm. It was more structured, supervised, and full of possibilities. But rules were rules, and the system had clear boundaries. Luke, despite the incredible talent everyone saw in him, could only train in boxing; he wasn't allowed to go professional until he turned eighteen and completed a proper education. Those were the conditions set to protect him, to make sure he didn't fall through the cracks as so many young fighters did.

The same guidelines applied to Steve, at least in terms of education. But football was different. The pathway for young talent was more flexible, and technically, Steve could go professional at any time if the right offer came. Still, their father insisted that both boys balance their abilities with schooling. It wasn't negotiable. "Talent can open doors," he often reminded them, "but education keeps you standing once you're on the other side."

There was something else, something even more important to Steve.

He wouldn't train without Luke. It was a rule that he simply refused to break, not for anything.

It didn't matter how big the opportunity was or how many scouts came around. If his brother wasn't at the pitch, Steve simply wasn't himself. He would stand still, hands by his sides, refusing to move until Luke was beside him. The coach tried everything. He tried talking, encouraging, and even bribing with snacks. But nothing ever worked. Eventually, it was agreed: whenever Luke wasn't in the boxing gym training himself, he would accompany Steve to football practice. Just his presence grounded Steve, as if the world made sense only when his brother was within reach.

Training became a family affair. Their foster father drove them every day without complaint, rain or shine. Mum packed their lunches, labelled with their names, even though the boys always swapped them. It was their quiet way of saying, "We are in this together."

As summer began to fade and the next football season approached, the buzz around Steve only grew louder and louder. Coaches were talking. Parents around the neighbourhood constantly murmured. Kids looked and pointed. Some even tried imitating the way Steve ran, the quirky steps he took before shooting, the way his foot seemed to kiss the ball rather than kick it.

The local football community hadn't seen anything like him in years.

By the time the opening match arrived, expectations were sky-high. Their opponents were the champions from the previous season. They were bigger, faster, older, and of course, considerably more experienced than he was. The stadium was packed for a youth game, more packed than anyone expected. Even Luke, who wasn't easily impressed, felt a rush of nerves as he sat in the stands.

The whistle blew, and the match kicked off. For nearly forty-five minutes, both teams fought with everything they had. Tackles flew. Passes zipped by. The crowd roared at every near miss. The scoreboard stayed frozen at 0–0, and frustration began creeping into the players' movements.

But the manager had an ace up his sleeve.

With ten seconds left before halftime, he called Steve over. The boy stood up, wiped his hands on his shorts, and glanced toward the stands, searching until he found Luke. Their eyes met. Luke nodded once. That was all Steve needed.

The second half had barely settled when Steve shifted into another gear. For ten minutes, it was as if the world slowed around him. He scored three goals. Three in just a matter of ten minutes. Each one was faster and cleaner than the last. The crowd went wild. Even the opposing coaches stared, wide-eyed, trying to understand how a boy his age could play with such grace and precision.

When the match ended, the scoreboard read **3–0**. All three goals from one boy.

"Wonderful!" his manager exclaimed, running across the pitch with both hands in the air. "Absolutely wonderful!"

But this game wasn't just about the crowd, the cheering parents, or the usual local teams. That day, several managers from rival clubs were watching. Word had spread, and they wanted to see the boy for themselves. They wanted to see what he was all about. They wanted to confirm the rumours or dismiss them, once and for all.

They left impressed... very impressed.

Within only two days, the club chairman received more offers than he had in the entire past decade combined. The numbers being proposed were almost unbelievable. Some clubs offered more for Steve alone than our club spent on its entire youth program each year. The chairman nearly dropped his phone while reading the emails.

But Steve wasn't going anywhere.

The club turned down every bid, no matter how tempting. They knew what they had. And they knew he wasn't ready to be uprooted again, not after everything he'd survived.

Throughout the season, Steve terrorised defences. His left foot danced, his right foot struck, and his mind worked faster than anyone else on the pitch. Some games were won before they even began, just by the fear he planted in the other team.

By season's end, they were champions. Now they were moving up into top-flight youth football.

With success came another storm of offers. Bigger clubs. Bigger money. Bigger pressure.

It was time for a conversation.

The chairman asked the manager to arrange a meeting with Steve and his parents.

When they arrived, the atmosphere felt heavy. Papers were stacked on the chairman's desk, each contract thicker than the last. Steve sat between his mum and dad, hands fidgeting nervously. Luke sat beside them, not invited but refusing to leave his brother alone. His brother, of course, preferred it that way as well.

"We've received several offers for Steve," the chairman began, leaning forward, "These offers come from the top clubs in the league. Look... these uh... these are teams that can give him more money than we ever could, if I am being very honest about it. And it is good money as well."

Steve's face crumpled immediately. "I'm okay! I already have lots of money now. I don't want to leave. Have I done something wrong? Am I in trouble?"

His voice broke, and tears spilt down his cheeks.

Dad placed a hand on his shoulder. "So, you don't want to leave, son?"

"No..." Steve sniffled. "I don't want to go."

Luke slid closer and wrapped an arm around him. He didn't say anything, but his presence said enough.

Dad turned to the chairman. "What can you offer him, then?"

The chairman straightened his papers. "We can increase his wage by an extra five thousand on top of what he already earns. This would make him the highest-paid player in the entire youth team."

"Yes!! Yes!!" Steve jumped up, nearly knocking over his chair. "I don't want to play for another team! You've been good to my family and me. I want to stay!"

His parents exchanged a long, grateful look. It was rare to see a child who understood loyalty this deeply, especially one who had every reason not to trust the world.

A new contract was drawn up that same day.

Steve signed it with his hands shaking from excitement. Luke stood behind him, smiling proudly, knowing this was only the beginning.

But beneath all the cheers, the interviews, the applause in the club hallways, one truth remained steady:

None of this would have meant anything to Steve if Luke weren't beside him.

The brothers had survived storms, strangers, and uncertainty. They had endured hunger, fear, and the cold nights in that old building with the old lady who had changed their lives.

Now, they were finally building something new. And they had money for once to build it and see it through.

And deep down, even though neither boy said it out loud, they both knew:

This was only the beginning of the road ahead.

Chapter 6

A few days later, the house phone rang while Dad was washing the dishes. He wiped his hands on a towel and picked up, expecting it to be the club or perhaps a neighbour. Instead, he heard the familiar voice of the manager on the other end, but there was something different about his usually cheery tone.

"Listen," the manager began, "I've just received news. Steve has been selected to play for his country."

Dad felt his chest swell with pride. National selection. It was the dream of every father whose child played a sport. "That's incredible. He'll be over the moon."

"Yes," the manager said slowly, "but... there's a snag. I need to confirm his place of birth to finish the paperwork."

Dad froze. Of course. The boys' backstory had always been murky, which is why this was a slightly concerning territory. Bits and pieces gathered from what the boys told them about their life with the old lady and from what the authorities could piece together. But official documentation? That was another matter.

"So, we need to contact Social Services," the manager continued. "I didn't think it would be an issue, but... well, it turns out it is."

Dad didn't like the sound of that.

Later that afternoon, he called their social worker, hoping for a straightforward answer. Instead, he was met with resistance the moment he mentioned Steve's selection.

"I can't release that information," the social worker said sharply. "Both boys have had little to no education. It already raises concerns. Before anything else is addressed, their lack of schooling must be resolved."

It wasn't just Steve. It was Luke as well. Two boys, talented beyond measure, but with gaps in their learning that no one had helped them fill.

Dad sighed heavily. "So, what do we do?"

"You do nothing," she replied coldly. "It's on us to decide their next steps."

Dad hung up feeling unsettled. But shortly afterwards, he called the manager again and explained everything. The manager didn't hesitate.

"It's time I make good on my promise," he said. "I'll arrange for them to receive an education."

"But they're too old for school now," Dad reminded him.

"I know. But homeschooling is still an option. Let me look into tutors.

If you're willing to drop them off at the training ground each day, I'll make sure they're taught properly, supervised, and brought home afterwards. We'll make it work."

Relief washed over Dad. At last, someone was helping rather than judging.

The plan was set. The boys were excited. Steve especially, because studying at the club meant staying close to his football dream, close to the pitches where he felt alive. Luke was eager, too, ready to learn and keep his brother company.

But the next morning, as they were getting ready, schoolbags on their backs, football boots in one, boxing handwraps in the other, a heavy knock boomed on the front door.

Dad opened it, and his heart sank. It was the Social Services.

Three workers stood in the doorway, one holding a clipboard, the other two already looking past him as though searching the house.

"We've come for the boys," the lead worker said.

Dad's voice tightened. "Why?"

"You haven't provided them with proper educational support," she replied. "Neither you nor your wife has arranged schooling, and you're both out working all day. This placement is no longer suitable. They need a home that can offer full-time supervision."

Before Dad could respond, Steve stepped forward from behind him.

"NO!" he shouted. "No, no, no! I'm not going anywhere! We have a mother and father here!"

His voice cracked with panic, raw and trembling. Luke grabbed his arm, eyes wide.

The social worker didn't even flinch. "Don't make this harder than it already is," she said coldly.

Dad felt helpless for a moment, but then instinct took over. He hurried to the phone, dialled the manager's number with shaking hands.

"They're here," he whispered urgently. "Social Services. They say they're taking the boys."

"What? Now? I'm coming immediately," the manager said. "Keep them there with you."

"I'll try, but she's already called the police. She got upset because Steve told her he wasn't going."

The manager swore under his breath. "Just hold them until I arrive."

It was too late.

Minutes later, two officers walked up the driveway and entered the house with the kind of artificial calm that makes your skin crawl.

"What's going on, lads?" one officer said lightly. "Come on now, the social workers are here to help you."

"No, we're not going!" both boys shouted in unison.

The officer sighed impatiently and reached out, grabbing Steve by the arm.

"Come on, lad. We don't have time for this."

Steve jerked away, eyes wide with terror. The officer grabbed him again, harder this time.

"Oh no. You don't have to do that!" Mum cried, stepping forward.

"Don't let them take me, Mum!" Steve sobbed, his voice barely recognisable.

But the officers didn't care. They pulled the boys toward the doorway while Mum clung to Luke until she was finally forced to let go. Both boys cried, calling for them as the officers led them down the driveway. Their screams echoed through the house long after the door closed.

When the manager arrived ten minutes later, Dad was standing in the living room, shaking, tears streaking down his face.

"They just took them," he said in a broken whisper. "They wouldn't listen to anyone. The social worker was the same. She'd already made her mind up. There was no compassion shown to the boys at all. None. It was like they were just numbers on a sheet of paper."

He sank into a chair. "Luke and Steve... they were heartbroken. I don't know how they'll react. I've never seen anything like it. It was disgusting."

"If you find out where they've been taken, please... please let us know."

The manager placed a hand on his shoulder. "Don't you worry. The club's solicitors will be all over this."

And they were.

The very next day, the manager called the foster parents. "We've arranged a meeting with the solicitors regarding what happened. We want you there."

"We'll be there," Dad said firmly. "Give us the time. My wife has already said she'll give up her job. If that's all the boys needed, why didn't they just tell us that?"

The meeting was scheduled for the following week.

Mum had already resigned from work. She didn't hesitate, not even for a second. The boys' wellbeing came before anything else. From the day she met them, she had loved them fiercely. She wasn't going to let them be dragged through the system again, not without a fight.

That evening, the manager called with another update.

"Steve hasn't spoken since they took him," he said quietly.

Mum's hand flew to her mouth. "No. No. They can't put my boys in that place again. They have a home here with us."

Dad felt something harden inside him. Enough was enough. He called the social worker's office directly and asked to speak to her supervisor.

When the supervisor came on the line, Dad explained everything to the smallest of details.

There was a long silence on the other end.

"They were taken?" the supervisor finally said. "I... I had no idea. She never reported that."

"What do you mean?" Dad demanded.

"We've had complaints about her before," the supervisor said gravely. "Leave this with me."

For the first time in days, Dad felt a small light of hope.

Chapter 7

—— ✦ ——

Several days passed. Each day felt longer than the last for Mother and Father, the anxiety of waiting gnawing at their hearts. Every morning, they woke expecting a call, hoping someone would say the boys were coming home, but the phone never rang. All they wanted, all they had ever wanted since the nightmare began, was to have Luke and Steve back where they belonged: home, safe, and loved.

The boys' absence was visibly noticeable in the house. Everything seemed to be quieter around them, and the rooms were empty all of a sudden. Mother would sit in the living room, staring out of the window, her hands folded in her lap, fingers twisting together, eyes red from sleepless nights. Father would walk the garden, hands deep in his pockets, stopping every so often as if the boys might appear behind the fence, just waiting for a game or a fight to break out between them as it often did in happier times.

Late that afternoon, as the golden light of the sun stretched across the pavement, the phone rang. Mother and Father exchanged a glance, a mixture of hope and fear written across their faces. Father picked it up.

"This is Mr. Thomson," the voice on the line said, formal but with a trace of warmth. "I'm calling from Social Services. It is good news. We have completed our investigation regarding the social worker who took Luke and Steve from you, and she is now officially on report. She can no longer make unilateral decisions to remove children from a loving, stable home. We are deeply sorry for the distress caused to the boys... and to you."

Mother and Father felt the tension drain from their shoulders, replaced by a cautious, trembling relief. Father leaned against the kitchen counter, gripping it tightly as if grounding himself. "Thank you. Thank you so much," he said, his voice shaking. "Can we... can we collect the boys now?"

"There is, however, one condition," the social worker continued. "They cannot participate in sports until they are eighteen, unless they are receiving proper education. This is to ensure their academic development is not neglected."

Father's hands clenched into fists. "We understand completely. That has already been arranged. Luke and Steve will be home-schooled. Steve's manager has set strict levels for his football training, and Luke's boxing trainer is following a similar program. Education comes first; we told the social worker at the time. It has all been organised."

The voice on the line softened. "That is acceptable. I will send you the address where the boys are currently staying. Please, go to them immediately. We want to resolve this as quickly as possible. I will call tonight to make sure the transition is smooth."

The call ended, leaving Mother and Father staring at each other, the words sinking in slowly, as if they could not quite believe what had just happened. For a moment, the house was silent, save for the ticking of the wall clock, each tick echoing the rhythm of their racing hearts.

"Are you ready?" Mother asked, her voice trembling with both excitement and relief.

Father nodded. "More than ready. Let's bring them home."

With the address programmed into the sat nav, they drove in tense anticipation, every red light a minor test of patience, every passing pedestrian a reminder of how long it had felt since the boys had been taken.

When they pulled up outside the home, Luke's sharp eyes spotted the familiar car first. "Steve," he whispered urgently, "come on! Mum and Dad are here!"

Steve ran to the window, pressing his face against the glass. "Where are they?" he asked, voice trembling with a mixture of hope and disbelief.

"They're just coming to the door now," Luke said, heart pounding.

In a heartbeat, Steve nearly pushed Luke over in his rush, tearing the door open before they could even hear footsteps. "Mum! Mum! Don't leave me! I will be good!" he cried, tears streaming down his cheeks.

Mother rushed forward, dropping to her knees and wrapping both boys in her arms. Father followed, holding Luke tightly against him, whispering reassurances that neither of them could quite process yet. The boys sobbed freely, releasing the grief, the fear, the hopelessness that had been building for days. Even the social workers observing from the edge of the room couldn't help but feel their own eyes sting with tears.

"Don't worry, boys," Mother whispered, smoothing Steve's hair back from his tear-streaked face. "You are coming home now. With your father and me. You are safe."

Steve looked up at her, eyes wide, searching for reassurance. "My mum's come for me! I knew she would! Luke, we need to be good, so they don't take us away again. I'm not going to play football; I want my mum and dad. If the football is going to mess with that, then I don't want to play at all."

Father's jaw dropped. "Who told you that it was because of football?" he asked, disbelief etched on his face.

"The social worker," Steve said quietly, the words heavy with conviction. "She said if I didn't train or focus on football properly, I wouldn't stay here with you."

"No, that is wrong, Steve," Father said firmly, kneeling to look him in the eyes. "It has nothing to do with football. Nothing at all. You are here because we love you and because this is where you belong."

Luke tugged gently on Steve's sleeve. "See, I told you everything's going to be okay," he said, trying to steady himself, though he was still shaking from relief.

The person in charge of the home, a tall man with a kind but serious expression, stepped forward. "I will be investigating this thoroughly," he said. "We'll speak with the social worker's supervisor and make sure this never happens again. Children should never have to experience what you two have gone through."

Mother nodded firmly, a fire burning in her eyes. "I will make sure of it. Nobody is going to take my boys from me again. They have a home now, and we are keeping it that way."

Father placed a hand on Steve's shoulder, steadying him. "You've both been very brave. Very brave, and we are proud of you. But now, we need to go home, and we need to heal."

The boys clung to their parents as they walked to the car. For the first time in what felt like weeks, they didn't have to look over their shoulders, didn't have to worry about a knock at the door or a stern voice telling them they had nowhere to go.

The journey home was quiet at first. Luke and Steve pressed their faces against the windows, taking in the familiar sights of their town, the corner shop, the park where they had played as children, the row of houses that had always felt like home.

When they pulled up outside their own house, the boys nearly tumbled out of the car in their excitement. Mother held out her arms. "Welcome home," she said softly, tears glistening in her eyes. "Welcome back."

Steve ran to the front door, fists pumping the air in victory. "Home! We're home! No one can take us away again!"

Mother knelt on the floor, gathering both boys into a hug. "We are going to make up for everything you've been through. From now on, this is your home. Always."

Father joined them, placing a protective arm around his wife and the boys. "And we're going to make sure everything that happens next— school, sports, life—it's all fair and safe. No one will ever come and take you away from us again."

Steve looked up at him, eyes wide. "Even football, Dad?"

Father smiled gently. "Even football. You'll train, you'll learn, you'll play, but only in a way that keeps you safe, and keeps you with us."

Chapter 8

—— ⭐ ——

A full week passed before they heard anything more.

For Luke and Steve, it was the longest week of their lives. Every knock at the door made Steve flinch. Every ringing phone sent Luke's stomach into knots. They were back home, safe in their beds again, but the memory of being dragged away still clung to them like a shadow that refused to fade.

Mother barely left the house. She wanted to be there every moment, just in case someone tried to take them again. Father kept his phone charged and within reach at all times. He trusted no one now, not after what they had been through.

On the eighth morning, a black car pulled up outside the house. Luke saw it first.

"Dad," he said quietly. "There's someone outside."

Father went to the window. A tall man in a suit stepped out of the car, holding a briefcase. He walked slowly to the door and knocked. The sound echoed loudly through the house. He opened the door.

"Mr Thomson?" the man asked.

"Yes."

"My name is David Harrington. I'm the head of regional safeguarding for Social Services. May I come in?"

Father hesitated for only a moment before stepping aside. "Of course. Please come in."

The boys stood at the bottom of the stairs, watching nervously.

"Can I speak to you and the boys, please?" the man asked gently.

"Yes, come on through," Dad said. "Boys, you too."

Luke and Steve exchanged a glance before walking into the living room. Steve stood close to Mum, gripping her sleeve.

"What's up, Dad?" Steve whispered.

"Nothing, son. Someone is here to talk to us," Dad replied calmly.

They all sat down.

Mr Harrington opened his briefcase and placed a folder on the coffee table. His expression was serious.

"I want to start by apologising," he said. "What happened to you should never have happened. You were taken unlawfully, without authorisation, without cause, and without proper safeguarding review."

Steve's grip tightened on his mother's arm.

Luke swallowed. "So... she lied?"

"Yes," Mr Harrington said. "She did far more than lie."

He took a deep breath.

"The social worker who removed you is currently suspended from duty. She is under criminal investigation for misconduct, abuse of power, corruption, and conspiracy."

The room went silent. Mother covered her mouth.

Father leaned forward. "Conspiracy?"

Mr Harrington nodded.

"She accepted a bribe. A very large one."

Steve's heart started pounding. "A bribe?"

"Yes. She was paid to remove you from this home and place you into temporary care so that another football club could gain direct access to you."

Luke stared at him. "You mean... another team wanted Steve?"

"That is exactly what happened," the man said. "A top-tier club offered her a significant sum of money to interfere with your placement. Their intention was to pressure you into signing with them by isolating you from your family."

Steve felt sick.

"They tried to steal me," he whispered.

Father stood up slowly. His hands were shaking.

"Who did this?" he demanded.

Mr Harrington hesitated. "At this stage, I'm not permitted to name the club publicly. But the police are investigating them alongside the social worker. Charges will be brought."

Mum's voice trembled. "What kind of charges?"

"Bribery. Corruption. Abuse of public office. Child endangerment. Coercion. And conspiracy to interfere with a legal guardianship."

Steve's knees felt weak.

"They took us because of football?" he said.

"They took you because you are valuable," the man said. "And someone wanted to own that future."

Luke clenched his fists. "We're not owned by anyone."

"No," Mr Harrington said firmly. "And that's why this will be prosecuted to the fullest extent of the law."

He stood and closed his folder.

"The Crown Prosecution Service has already approved charges. The police will be making arrests. This will go to court. And I promise you, what happened to you will never be allowed to happen again."

Mother began to cry quietly.

Father rubbed his face. "I can't believe this... They put my boys through hell for money."

Mr Harrington placed a hand over his heart. "I am truly sorry. On behalf of the department, I apologise."

When he stood to leave, he turned back to the boys.

"You are safe now. And you are not alone."

After he left, the house sat in stunned silence.

Then Father reached for his phone.

"I'm calling the manager," he said.

The line rang twice before it was answered.

"Hello?"

"It's me," Father said. "You need to hear this."

When he finished explaining, there was a long pause on the other end.

Then the manager exploded.

"They bribed a social worker?" he shouted. "They tried to traffic a child through the care system?"

"Yes."

"That's criminal. That's beyond football. That's human exploitation."

The manager's voice hardened.

"I'm taking this to the FA. To UEFA. To FIFA. I'm going public with this if they don't act."

Father nodded even though the man couldn't see him. "We just want to protect the boys."

"And you will," the manager said. "But make no mistake. Just like the social worker, this club will also be punished. They've crossed a line no one should ever cross."

That evening, the chairman arrived in person.

He sat at the kitchen table, staring at the boys with deep concern.

"What they did to you is unforgivable," he said. "I've been in football for forty years. I've seen greed. I've seen corruption. But I've never seen anyone try to steal a child."

Steve looked down. "They scared us."

"I know," the chairman said gently. "And I swear to you, nothing like that will ever happen again."

He slid an envelope across the table.

"There's a cheque inside. Enough for you to move house. Somewhere private. Somewhere safe. Somewhere no one can find you."

Mother's eyes widened. "We can't take that."

"You can," he said firmly. "And you will. Because your family deserves peace."

Then he turned to Steve.

"There is only one condition."

Steve tensed.

"I want you to sign a contract with us. A proper one. One that protects you. One that guarantees your family's safety. We will put lawyers on it. Safeguards. Protection clauses. And full education support."

Steve looked at his parents. "Mum, will you help me?"

"Yes," Mum said instantly. "You don't sign anything yet. Your dad and I will read it. We'll speak to lawyers. We'll take our time."

The chairman nodded. "That's exactly what I want."

Father placed a hand on Steve's shoulder. "You don't owe anyone anything, son. Not your talent. Not your future. You choose what happens next."

Steve nodded slowly.

"I just want to play football," he said. "And have my family."

The chairman smiled. "Then that's exactly what we'll protect."

Later that night, Luke and Steve lay in their beds, staring at the ceiling.

"They tried to buy us," Steve whispered.

"They didn't win," Luke said.

Steve turned to him. "Do you think we're safe now?"

Luke nodded. "We're not alone anymore. That's the difference."

Downstairs, Mum and Dad sat together, holding hands.

"They messed with the wrong family," Mum said quietly.

Father nodded. "And now they're going to pay for it."

Chapter 9

The boys were finally back home. Back where they belonged.

Steve lay on his bed staring at the ceiling, listening to the sound of his mother moving around in the kitchen downstairs, the familiar clink of cups and plates bringing him a comfort he had almost forgotten. Luke sat on the edge of his own bed, arms folded, a small smile on his face.

"See, Steve," Luke said. "I told you Mum and Dad would come back for us."

Steve turned his head and grinned. "Yeah. You always know better than me."

Luke stood up and ruffled his brother's hair. "That's because I'm your big brother. I'll always look out for you."

Steve laughed. "You always have."

Luke went quiet for a while after that, watching the light spill across the garden, and for a moment, he let himself remember what it had once been like. He remembered the nights spent curled up in doorways, the hunger that gnawed at his stomach, the fear of not knowing where they would sleep or whether tomorrow would be any kinder than today. He remembered holding Steve close under rain-soaked cardboard, promising him that things would get better even when he didn't believe it himself. To stand here now, under a real roof, in a real home, with parents who loved them and a future that finally felt solid, filled his chest with a gratitude so deep it almost hurt. Life had given them a second chance, and Luke swore to himself he would never waste it.

Downstairs, Mum stood by the window watching them through the glass reflection, her heart full. She had never imagined life would bring her two sons like this. She kissed Dad on the cheek as he passed her a cup of tea.

"They're home," she whispered. "That's all that matters."

Steve bounded down the stairs moments later.

"Mum, when can we go back to the training ground?"

Mum folded her arms and smiled. "Hold your horses, Steve. Your dad and I missed you. Can we have this weekend as a family first?"

Steve paused for a moment before nodding enthusiastically. "Yeah. That sounds great."

That weekend, they did all the small things that felt enormous. They went for walks. They cooked together. They watched films on the sofa with Luke hogging the blanket. They laughed. They talked. They healed. They tried their best to put everything that had happened behind them. It did not matter anymore. They were together, and they were safe. That is all that mattered.

For the first time in a long time, Steve slept through the night. He slept soundly and woke up feeling like a baby, like someone born anew, fresh and energised. A week later, he was back at training.

The manager watched him from the touchline, shaking his head in disbelief. Even after everything he had been through, Steve played as if nothing could touch him. The ball moved where he wanted it. His feet danced across the grass. His confidence was quiet but unbreakable.

"We need to get this schoolwork sorted," the manager said to the education coordinator. "He needs to be playing next week."

"I've spoken to his dad. Social services are fine with it. Steve and Luke have reached a level that's acceptable."

The manager smiled. "Great. He's playing Saturday in the cup match."

The anticipation spread through the club like wildfire.

Steve had trained well before, but now he was starting.

The stands sold out in hours.

Fans arrived early, wearing shirts with his name printed on the back. Children lined the tunnel, hoping to see him walk out. Pundits buzzed with excitement. The stadium roared when Steve stepped onto the pitch.

He closed his eyes for a moment, breathing in the sound. Luke sat beside Dad in the stands, fists clenched in pride.

"Go on, little brother," Luke whispered.

The whistle blew.

The ball moved quickly across the pitch. Steve's team kept possession, moving with purpose. Then the ball came to him. The crowd rose as one.

Steve glided forward. He slipped past one defender, then another. A nutmeg. A step-over. A feint. The ball never left his control.

The commentators could barely keep up.

"Look at his composure."

"He plays like he's been here for ten years."

"Is that ball glued to his foot?"

Steve cut inside and fired.

Top corner.

The stadium erupted.

He ran to the corner flag, arms raised, eyes wide with disbelief.

Then he did it again.

And again.

And again.

By halftime, he had scored five goals and assisted two.

Seven-nil.

The manager pulled him aside as the players walked off.

"That's enough for today, son."

Steve blinked. "Did I do okay?"

The manager laughed. "You were perfect."

The game finished 7–2. The cup run continued.

The reporters waited.

But the manager shielded him.

The club captain stood in front of the cameras instead.

"We wanted to speak to Steve," a reporter said.

"I know," the captain replied. "But he's a bit young for that. He needs protecting."

"Which country will he play for?"

The captain shrugged. "That's a story for another day. For now, just enjoy watching him."

The season restarted.

Steve played most of the matches in the first half.

They were unbeaten.

But his parents noticed the tiredness creeping into his eyes. The late nights studying. The strain of expectations. Social services stepped in.

"He's too young to be playing every week," they said. "He needs rest."

The manager had no choice. Steve was told no more football for the rest of the season.

At first, he was devastated. But then the phone rang.

It was Father.

"They've found your birth certificates."

Steve froze.

"What?"

"You and Luke turn eighteen in two weeks."

Everything changed in that moment.

But Steve looked at his mum.

"We'll wait," he said. "We'll finish school first. That's what we promised."

The manager respected the decision.

The fans waited.

Now it was Luke's turn.

Luke walked into the boxing gym, as he belonged there. His shoulders were broader now. His eyes were sharper. His fists were faster. Now it was his turn to shine. To put all of the skills he had acquired through his hard days to the test. To actually practice the art of discipline and control through jabs and hooks and slipping past opponents. To see the beauty in movement, the beauty in hitting and not getting hit. The beauty in practising an art form that was nothing short of meditation.

His trainer watched him spar for the first time and shook his head.

"Where did you learn to fight like that?"

Luke smiled. "The streets." And that was the bare truth of it. He did learn to fight in the actual world, not in air-conditioned gymnasiums. He knew what it meant to fight. More importantly, he knew how important it was to know when to fight and when not to. Within weeks, people were talking. The two brothers were suddenly the talk of the town and beyond. The young prodigies were ready to dominate their individual sports.

Then a champion called him out. He was a belt-holder and a professional.

The gym buzzed.

Luke's dad was worried.

"It's too soon."

Luke shook his head. "Dad, I've been fighting my whole life. I protected Steve when we had nothing. I protected our mum. The old lady taught me everything. This is what I was born for."

Dad looked at him and saw the boy who had carried his brother across rain-soaked streets, who had stolen bread to survive, who had never once turned his back on family.

He nodded.

"I trust you."

The fight was arranged, and the future was set.

That night, Steve and Luke stood in the garden under the stars.

"You're going to be champion," Steve said.

Luke smirked. "So are you."

Steve grinned. "We made it."

Luke looked at him seriously. "We survived."

Steve nodded. "Together."

Inside the house, Mum watched them from the window. Her heart was entirely full of love and admiration for her boys. The boys often expressed how grateful they were for how much she had given them. But little did they know that it was incomparable to how much they had given her. Only a mother could understand and articulate that feeling.

Two boys who had nothing. Now I have everything. They had family. They had purpose. They had the will to live and not just survive. They had things to look forward to. And most importantly, they had people at home who loved them and looked forward to seeing them thrive every day.

They had a destiny that no one could steal, not anymore.